This book is dedicated to my amazing students at Mighty Oaks Academy who brought joy to my life during the 2024/2025 school year

ISBN: 978-1-962737-27-2

Published by 3 R Press 2025

This book is a collection of explanatory, or "how-to" essays written and illustrated by the second and third grade students in Mrs. Baker's class at Mighty Oaks Academy, in February of 2025.

Do you find yourself watching cat videos? Do you want a cat? Fun fact: cats are loyal felines! Taking care of a cat is easy if you know the right steps. First, you need food, water, cat toys, litter box, and a cat if you don't have one and your cat needs this. Second, you need to give your cat a lot of attention and it will start to like you. Third, you need a scoop with lines and holes then scoop the litter box and put it in a bag. Put the bag in the trash. Finally, you pour water in one of the bowls and fill the other bowl, you need half a

cup of catfood. There you go! Now you know

how to take care of a cat!

Payton 3rd grade

Did you know people have been playing football for over 156 years? Playing football is easyier if you know the rules. First, get a football that you will be comfortable throwing, catching and kicking Then, have some one throw it to you and then make a dimamond with your thumbs and pointer fingers crossed line your hands up with the ball. Once the ball hits you squize it a little bit. The next thing is punting. Punting is when you hold the the ball in front of you then drop it and try to kick it. You can punt the ballwhen it's fourth down or when you get tackled in your own end zone. Another thing is fouls. A comon foul is offsides. Offsides is when you pass the line of scrimmage. Befor the ball is snapped. The line of scrimmish is the exact yard line the ball was the play before. Another common foul is holding. Holding is when you hold someone for too long. Over time is a comon thing. Over time is not a foul. It is when the clock runs out in the fourth quarter and the game is tied. One more thing is pass interference. Pass interference is when you push your defender or your defender pushes you. If you can I would make sure you're in good shape because football is a tough and contact sport. Two of the most comman football leagues are the NFL and college football. There is also flag football, two hand touch, and one hand touch. Flag, football is where you wear flags and you try to pull the flag off the person with the ball. Two hand touch is where you try to touch the guy with the ball same with one hand touch. Football is only played in the U.S.A. Football is not an olympic sport. The first seventeen games are normal season games the next two play off games, and the last game is the Super Bowl. The next thing is downs. Downs are plays and you have four downs and if you get a first down. Now that you know somethings about football, have some fun. Remember, practice makes perfect.

Briggs grade 3

Do you know one of the easiest lunch? I know, it's a peanut butter and jelly sandwich. The sandwich became popular during the Great Depression. Making a peanut butter and jelly sandwich is easy if you know the steps. First, prepare your ingredients, which are bread, jam, peanut butter and a knife. Then, prepare the bread, open the bag of bread. Then put the jam one side, open the jar and grab the spoon and put some on the spoon, then put it on one side. After, put the peanut butter on the other bread, open the peanut butter jar and grab the knife, put some peanut butter on the knife then spread it on the other pices of bread and grab the two pices of and put them together. And now you know how to make a peanut butter jam sandwich. By Elizabeth C. Second grade

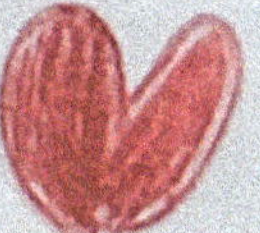
Yummy!

DO you know how to make a pizza? PIZZa was invented in the city of Naples, Italy, in the 1800s. Making pizza is very easy if you know the right steps. You goto the store and you get fresh dough you go back home and you spread the pizza souse on the pizza put peper and onions on the pizza and then you put it in the oven for 20 min. when the pizza is in the oven you let it wait for 20min. When it is done you pull it out. you can make another if your mom lets you when it comes out of the oven it is vary hot wait for it to cool down and then you can eat it when the pizza is cooked. Pizza is easy if you know the write steps.

Lane 3rd

homemade pizza
pizza dough
tomato paste
pepperoni

Have you ever seen funny dog videos? Do you want to be that person taking the video? Then get a dog! Taking care of a dog is easy if you know the right steps. First, you get your things to take care of a dog, like food, water, some toys like a ball, and of course a dog. Make sure you name your dog. A dog might not play with its toys so make sure you play with it. A dog can entertain you for hours or even years! Next, dogs like to play catch or just chase you around. Dogs just like to run around for the most part. Dogs also love to sleep with you but sometimes it can be annoying to sleep with them every night. So you might want to get a bed for it to sleep in. Don't forget to feed the dog every day with a scoop of dog food twice a day, morning and night. You also need to put water from a cup or hose once a day. Fill the water to the top of the bowl. Last, but not least, here is a thing that you might not want to do but it is a part of taking care of a dog. You have to pick up after your dog like when dog goes to the bathroom or when it chews up things. So what do think? Do you want a cute, funny, and entertaining dog? Well you learned how to take care of one!

By: Swayzee D.   grade 3

Wrestling is a good sport because you can get stronger. I learned how to do a cradle, a move in wrestling, which I learned when I was five. With just three steps and do the steps right, you a ? Bow and arrow cradle. First, you get in your stance and take them down and grab their leg and head then push then you look your hands. A stance is when you squat down with your head up. Next, you shoot for your opponent's legs then circle around them then you get three points. If you are down on the bottom and you get out of it, is one point since you learned how to wrestle you can enjoy the sport, wrestling is a good sport because you can get stronger.

Bodie H. gread 2

Are you hungry? Well, I've got a snack for you! It's a bread bear! It is easy if you know the steps. These are the ingredients: a slice of bread, three tiny slices of banana, three blueberries (make sure you washed them), and peanut butter. First put a little peanut butter on top. Then put the two slices of banana near the end of the slice of bread. Next put a banana in the middle. Last put the two blueberries under the ears and put the last blueberry on top of the middle. Enjoy!

Maya   grade 2

Have you ever tried to care for your own small or big dog? It' easy if you know the right steps. First you get up get ready. Next, you eat breakfast then, get a dog bowl and use a dog scooper and scoop up dog food for example: my dog's names are Zuzu and Daisy and I have to do a amount of food so I don't get it to spill when they eat. Then, you stack the dog bowls and bring it to them and say sit.

Then you pray for them like "Dear
God, please make sure that my dog is
healthy for my dog so he or she does
not get sick, in Jesus' Name Amen."
And then you tell the dogs eat and
they dogs eat. So that's how
you feed your dog! Now,
if they get dirty? You have
to clean them. This is how you
clean them and not only cleaning
you need to walk them and
clean them so it doesn't stain
and get all over your house and make sure
that you bring dog bags so they don't go some where

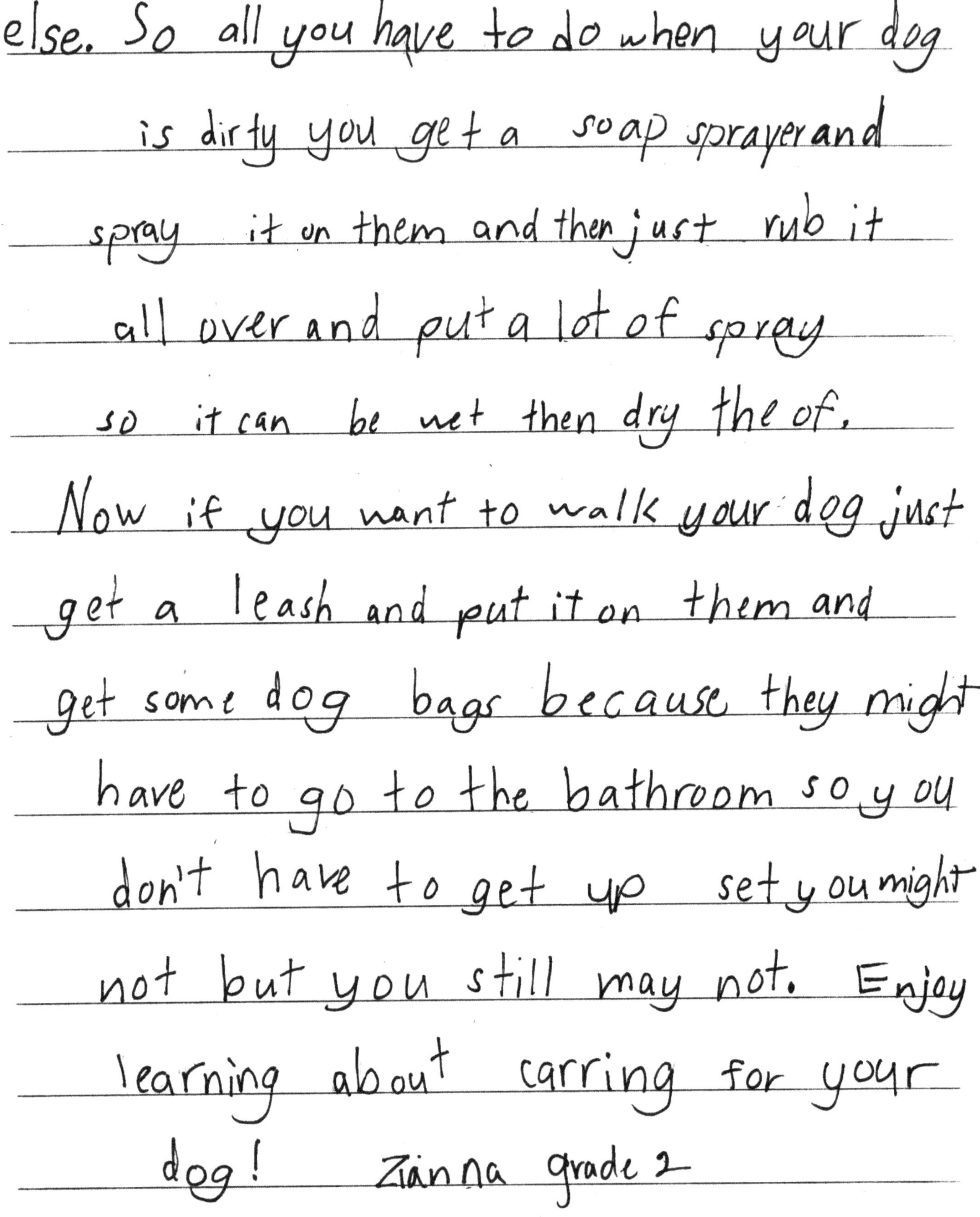

else. So all you have to do when your dog is dirty you get a soap sprayer and spray it on them and then just rub it all over and put a lot of spray so it can be wet then dry the of. Now if you want to walk your dog just get a leash and put it on them and get some dog bags because they might have to go to the bathroom so you don't have to get up set you might not but you still may not. Enjoy learning about carring for your dog! Zianna grade 2

What goes good with chips? Fortnite! People have been making video games for years. Video games are easy if you know the right steps. First, Get a PS4 or a PS5 and a nintedo. Second, Get a controller the x buttun makes you jump. R2 makes you shoot. R1 makes you aim. Then, Get a friend on the game and if you play for a long time you become a pro. Then you can play Battle royle to ready up you press ∆ to ready up.

You press Ⓧ to get out of the battle bus. You can play Rebad, Zero Build, OG, Super red vs blue and lvl you can play with your friend or without your friends. Now you know how to play Fortnite.

Harley grade 3

If you're bored at recess, play Four Square! Playing four square is easy if you know the right steps. First, you get a ball that can bounce, make sure you pump up the ball if you need to. Then, you mark four big squares. Each square should be 8ft. by 8ft, at least. Find five or more people. One of squares is king, one is queen, one is knight, and another is peasant. Nest, if your in king, you bounce the ball in your square once and hit the ball, in someone in queen, knight, or peasant. Then, they hit it to someone in the squares and just keep hitting it. Then, if the ball bounces twice in your square, your out, and you replace players. Last, you can play as many rounds as you want, and now you know how to play Four Square!

By: Milli   3rd grade

Do you know that wrestling is the most contact sport? It's called that because you basically hit someone. So, we're going to learn a wrestling move called a sweep single. But you need to learn to do the steps and do them right you can do a sweep single. So first you get in your stance and circle away from the leg that you're going to attack. Next you grab the leg that you were circling away from. Last, stand up and trip your apponent.

Now you can defend yourself by using a wrestling move called the sweep single.

Ashton 3rd grade

Do you like getting medals?
you can earn medals in wrestling.
Wrestling is one of the oldest
sports in the world, with cave
drawings depicting, or showing
wrestling, as far back as 3,000
B.C. wrestling is easy.

Do you know how to wrestle?
the wrestling stance is popular?
Learning
the rules will be easy maybe.
Get you wrestling shoes on and
tie them. Why you need certain
shoes is because it will get on the
and when you wrestle you can get
medals and then you'll be done.
Tyler second grade

Do you know, How to take care of horses? If you know the right steps. Horses need alfalfa and bermuda hay. Feed them a whole flake and salt. They live in a pen and you can ride them pet them and put the food in the black bucket. Put the saddle on the horse and that is how to take care of horses.

Ananiah 2 grade

I am
good feedeing
horsisand
apig and
apones
and bmoode
and a lfafe.

"How to Play Basketball"   Name Parker

Have you ever played basketball?
Basketball is a good sport for you because you can get
all of your energy out because you get to run!
You have to practice dribbling. You have to
priactice dribbling because there are kids around
and tring to get the ball. First, you have to get a
basketball and practice dribbling. Why you need
to practice dribbling because there are kids around
and trying to get the ball. Then, you have to
practice shooting the ball in the hoop. The reason
you need to practice is because if you
shoot the ball into the hoop and make it you
get two points, the team with the most points wins!
Next, you have to practice runing fast, because
you have to get down the court fast. Last, you have
to practice passing. You pass because you have to get
theball to your teamate. With all of these things put
together you will learn the sport of basketball.

SPALDING
Parker

Do you like the thrill of riding fast? Riding a dirt bike is easy if you know the right steps. First you check the gas. There's nothing worse than running out of gas. Now that your tank is full you get on the dirt bike then put on your Helmet — remember safety first. So now you kick start your engine. Lastly twist the throttle and have fun. Tabias grade 2

we hope you enjoyed learning about the
easy steps to doing things in life
(according to second and third graders).

Our prayer is that you will be inspired
to try something new.

"Let us not become weary in doing good, for at the proper time
we will reap a harvest if we do not give up." Galatians 6:9